Services Marketing

and

Social Marketing

:: Author ::

Prakash Parmar
(M.Com., B.ed.,NET., M.B.A)

PUBLISHED BY

The New Era International Publishing House
HQ. At & Po. Chaveli., Ta- Chansma,
Dist- Patan, North Gujarat, India, Asia.
www.iphouseindia.com

First Publication: 24rd March, 2015

ISBN:- 978-15-08949-90-9

Price: Rs.800/- INDIA

$ 15 OUTSIDE INDIA

PUBLISHED BY

**The New Era International Publishing House
HQ. At & Po. Chaveli., Ta- Chansma,
Dist- Patan, North Gujarat, India, Asia.
www.iphouseindia.com**

Services Marketing - Definition and Characteristics

Introduction

The world economy nowadays is increasingly characterized as a service economy. This is primarily due to the increasing importance and share of the service sector in the economies of most developed and developing countries. In fact, the growth of the service sector has long been considered as indicative of a country's economic progress.

Economic history tells us that all developing nations have invariably experienced a shift from agriculture to industry and then to the service sector as the main stay of the economy.

This shift has also brought about a change in the definition of goods and services themselves. No longer are goods considered separate from services. Rather, services now increasingly represent an integral part of the product and this interconnectedness of goods and services is represented on a goods-services continuum.

Definition and characteristics of Services

The American Marketing Association defines services as - "Activities, benefits and satisfactions which are offered for sale or are provided in connection with the sale of goods."

The defining characteristics of a service are:

Intangibility: Services are intangible and do not have a physical existence. Hence services cannot be touched, held, tasted or smelt. This is most defining feature of a service and that which primarily differentiates it from a product. Also, it poses a unique challenge to those engaged in marketing a service as they need to attach tangible attributes to an otherwise intangible offering.

1. **Heterogeneity/Variability:** Given the very nature of services, each service offering is unique and cannot be exactly repeated even by the same service provider. While products can be mass produced and be homogenous the same is not true of services. E.g. All burgers of a particular flavor at McDonalds are almost identical. However, the same is not true of the service rendered by the same counter staff consecutively to two customers.

2. **Perish ability :** Services cannot be stored, saved, returned or resold once they have been used. Once rendered to a customer the service is completely consumed and cannot be delivered to another

customer. E.g. A customer dissatisfied with the services of a barber cannot return the service of the haircut that was rendered to him. At the most he may decide not to visit that particular barber in the future.

3. **Inseparability/Simultaneity of production and consumption:** This refers to the fact that services are generated and consumed within the same time frame. E.g. a haircut is delivered to and consumed by a customer simultaneously unlike, say, a takeaway burger which the customer may consume even after a few hours of purchase. Moreover, it is very difficult to separate a service from the service provider. E.g. the barber is necessarily a part of the service of a haircut that he is delivering to his customer.

Types of Services

1. **Core Services:** A service that is the primary purpose of the transaction. E.g. a haircut or the services of lawyer or teacher.

2. **Supplementary Services:** Services that are rendered as a corollary to the sale of a tangible product. E.g. Home delivery options offered by restaurants above a minimum bill value.

Difference between Goods and Services

Given below are the fundamental differences between physical goods and services:

Goods	Services
A physical commodity	A process or activity
Tangible	Intangible
Homogenous	Heterogeneous
Production and distribution are separation from their consumption	Production, distribution and consumption are simultaneous processes
Can be stored	Cannot be stored
Transfer of ownership is possible	Transfer of ownership is not possible

Services Marketing - Definition and its Importance

Stated simply, Services Marketing refers to the marketing of services as against tangible products.

As already discussed, services are inherently intangible, are consumed simultaneously at the time of their production, cannot be stored, saved or resold once they have been used and service offerings are unique and cannot be exactly repeated even by the same service provider.

Marketing of services is a relatively new phenomenon in the domain of marketing, having gained in importance as a discipline only towards the end of the 20th century.

Services marketing first came to the fore in the 1980's when the debate started on whether marketing of services was significantly different from that of products so as to be classified as a separate discipline. Prior to this, services were considered just an aid to the production and marketing of goods and hence were not deemed as having separate relevance of their own.

The 1980's however saw a shift in this thinking. As the service sector started to grow in importance and emerged as a significant employer and contributor to the GDP, academics and marketing practitioners began to look at the marketing of services in a new light. Empirical research was conducted which brought to light the specific distinguishing characteristics of services. By the mid 1990's, Services Marketing was firmly entrenched as a significant sub discipline of marketing with its own empirical research and data and growing significance in the increasingly service sector dominated economies of the new millennium. New areas of study opened up in the field and were the subject of extensive empirical research giving rise to concepts such as - the product-service spectrum, relationship marketing, franchising of services, customer retention etc.

Importance of Marketing of Services

Given the intangibility of services, marketing them becomes a particularly challenging and yet extremely important task.

- **A key differentiator:** Due to the increasing homogeneity in product offerings, the attendant services provided are emerging as a key differentiator in the mind of the consumers. E.g. In case of two fast food chains serving a similar product (Pizza Hut and Domino's), more than the product it is the service quality that distinguishes the two brands from each other. Hence, marketers can leverage on the service offering to differentiate themselves from the competition and attract consumers.

- **Importance of relationships:** Relationships are a key factor when it comes to the marketing of services. Since the product is intangible, a large part of the customers' buying decision will depend on the degree to which he trusts the seller. Hence, the need to listen to the needs of the customer and fulfill them through the appropriate service offering and build a long lasting relationship which would lead to repeat sales and positive word of mouth.

- **Customer Retention:** Given today's highly competitive scenario where multiple providers are vying for a limited pool of customers, retaining customers is even more important than attracting new ones. Since services are usually generated and consumed at the same time, they actually involve the customer in service delivery process by taking into consideration his requirements and feedback. Thus they offer greater scope for customization according to customer requirements thus offering increased satisfaction leading to higher customer retention.

The 7 P's of Services Marketing

The first four elements in the services marketing mix are the same as those in the traditional marketing mix. However, given the unique nature of services, the implications of these are slightly different in case of services.

1. **Product:** In case of services, the 'product' is intangible, heterogeneous and perishable. Moreover,

its production and consumption are inseparable. Hence, there is scope for customizing the offering as per customer requirements and the actual customer encounter therefore assumes particular significance. However, too much customization would compromise the standard delivery of the service and adversely affect its quality. Hence particular care has to be taken in designing the service offering.

2. **Pricing:** Pricing of services is tougher than pricing of goods. While the latter can be priced easily by taking into account the raw material costs, in case of services attendant costs - such as labor and overhead costs - also need to be factored in. Thus a restaurant not only has to charge for the cost of the food served but also has to calculate a price for the ambience provided. The final price for the service is then arrived at by including a mark up for an adequate profit margin.

3. **Place:** Since service delivery is concurrent with its production and cannot be stored or transported, the location of the service product assumes importance. Service providers have to give special thought to where the service would be provided. Thus, a fine

dine restaurant is better located in a busy, upscale market as against on the outskirts of a city. Similarly, a holiday resort is better situated in the countryside away from the rush and noise of a city.

4. **Promotion:** Since a service offering can be easily replicated promotion becomes crucial in differentiating a service offering in the mind of the consumer. Thus, service providers offering identical services such as airlines or banks and insurance companies invest heavily in advertising their services. This is crucial in attracting customers in a segment where the services providers have nearly identical offerings.

We now look at the 3 new elements of the services marketing mix - people, process and physical evidence - which are unique to the marketing of services.

5. **People:** People are a defining factor in a service delivery process, since a service is inseparable from the person providing it. Thus, a restaurant is known as much for its food as for the service provided by its staff. The same is true of banks and department stores. Consequently, customer service training for

staff has become a top priority for many organizations today.

6. **Process:** The process of service delivery is crucial since it ensures that the same standard of service is repeatedly delivered to the customers. Therefore, most companies have a service blue print which provides the details of the service delivery process, often going down to even defining the service script and the greeting phrases to be used by the service staff.

7. **Physical Evidence:** Since services are intangible in nature most service providers strive to incorporate certain tangible elements into their offering to enhance customer experience. Thus, there are hair salons that have well designed waiting areas often with magazines and plush sofas for patrons to read and relax while they await their turn. Similarly, restaurants invest heavily in their interior design and decorations to offer a tangible and unique experience to their guests.

Services Marketing - Moment of Truth

Every business knows that in order to thrive it needs to differentiate itself in the mind of the consumer. Price has proved inadequate since there is a limit to how much a firm can cut back on its margins. Product differentiation is also no longer enough to attract or retain customers since technological advances have resulted in products becoming almost identical with very few tangible differences from others in the same category. Consequently, marketers have realized the importance of service differentiation as a sustainable strategy for competing for a portion of the customer's wallet.

Service Encounter / Moment of Truth

A moment of truth is usually defined as an instance wherein the customer and the organization come into contact with one another in a manner that gives the customer an opportunity to either form or change an impression about the firm. Such an interaction could occur through the product of the firm, its service offering or both. Various instances could constitute a moment of truth - such as greeting the customer, handling customer queries or complaints, promoting special offers or giving discounts and the closing of the interaction.

Importance

In today's increasingly service driven markets and with the proliferation of multiple providers for every type of product or service, moments of truth have become an important fact of customer interaction that marketers need to keep in mind. They are critical as they determine a customer's perception of, and reaction to, a brand. Moments of truth can make or break an organization's relationship with its customers.

This is more so in the case of service providers since they are selling intangibles by creating customer expectations. Services are often differentiated in the minds of the customer by promises of what is to come. Managing these expectations constitutes a critical component of creating favorable moments of truth which in turn are critical for business success.

Moments of Magic and Moments of Misery

Moments of Magic: Favorable moments of truth have been termed as 'moments of magic'. These are instances where the customer has been served in a manner that exceeds his expectations. E.g. An airline passenger being upgraded to from an economy to a business class ticket or the 100th (or 1000th) customer of a new department store being given a special discount on his purchase. Such gestures can go a long way in creating a regular and loyal customer base. However, a moment of magic need not necessarily involve such grand gestures. Even the efficient and timely service consistently provided by the coffee shop assistant can create a moment of magic for the customers.

Moment of Misery: These are instances where the customer interaction has a negative outcome. A delayed flight, rude and inattentive shop assistants or poor quality of food served at a restaurant all qualify as moments of misery for the customers. Though lapses in service cannot be totally avoided, how such a lapse is handled can go a long way in converting a moment of misery in to a moment of magic and creating a lasting impact on the customer.

Customer's Expectations and Delight
Introduction

In today's ultra competitive business environment merely meeting customer expectations is not enough. In order to effectively differentiate themselves from the competition, service providers need to focus on exceeding customer expectations to create customer delight and create a pool of loyal customers. Therefore, when deciding on a service delivery design, it is imperative for the service provider to consider the targeted customer base and their needs and expectations. This will help in developing a service design that will help the provider to effectively manage customer expectations leading to customer delight.

Customer Needs and Expectations

Customer needs comprise the basic reason or requirement that prompts a customer to approach a service provider. For instance, a person visits a restaurant primarily for the food it serves. That is the customer's need. However, the customer expects polite staff, attentive yet non intrusive service and a pleasant ambience. If these expectations are not properly met the guest would leave the restaurant dissatisfied even if his basic requirement of a meal being served has been met. Thus knowing and understanding guest expectations is important for any service provider.

Customer Satisfaction, Dissatisfaction and Delight

Based on the quality of the service experience a customer will either be satisfied, dissatisfied or delighted. Knowing a customer's expectation is instrumental in developing a strategy for meeting and exceeding customer expectations.

1. **Customer Dissatisfaction:** This is a situation when the service delivery fails to match up to the customer's expectations. The customer does not perceive any value for money. It's a moment of misery for the customer.

2. **Customer Satisfaction:** In this case, the service provider is able to match the customer's expectations and deliver a satisfactory experience. However, such a customer is not strongly attached to the bran and may easily shift to a competing brand for considerations of price or discounts and freebies.

3. **Customer Delight:** This is an ideal situation where the service provider is able to exceed the customer's expectations creating a Moment of Magic for the customer. Such customers bond with the brand, are regular and loyal and will not easily shift to other brands.

Meeting and Exceeding Customer Expectations

Exceeding customer expectations is all about creating that extra value for the customer. The hospitality industry specializes in creating customer delight.

Example, most 5 star hotels maintain customer databases detailing room order choices of their guests. So if a guest has asked for say orange juice to be kept in the mini bar in his room, the next time that he makes a reservation at the hotel, the staff ensures that the juice s already kept in the room. Such small gestures go a long way in making customers feel important and creating customer delight.

Another novel way of exceeding guest expectations is often demonstrated by travel companies. Since, they usually have details on their customers' birthdays, they often send out an email greeting to their guests to wish them. This not only makes an impact on the guest but also helps to keep the company acquire 'top of the mind recall' with the guest.

Maintaining Service Quality

After having attained the desired service level, the next great challenge faced by service providers is to maintain service standards at levels of excellence. This is as important, and as tough, as establishing service standards and attaining to them in the first place.

There are basically two approaches that any organization can have towards maintaining service standards - a proactive approach or a reactive approach.

Proactive: A proactive approach entails actively reaching out to customers and trying to gather their feedback on service quality and suggested areas of improvement. This can be done by way of

- Surveys and administering questionnaires
- Gap Analysis, and
- Staff training

a. **Surveys and questionnaires:** Such an approach helps a brand to anticipate customer demands and expectations and align its service offering accordingly. Also, the findings of such surveys can help to identify common issues and demands of customers hence helping a company to customize its service offering.

b. **Gap Analysis:** Another approach that is adopted for analyzing service quality is that of the gap analysis. The company has an ideal service standard that it would like to offer to its customers. This is contrasted with the current level of service being offered. The gap thus identified serves both as a measure and as a basis for planning a future course of action to improve the service offering.

c. **Staff Training:** Another crucial aspect of the proactive approach is staff training. Companies nowadays spend generously on training their personnel to adequately handle customer queries and/or complaints. This is particularly true if a company is changing its service offering or going in for a price hike of its existing services. For example, when a fast food chain increases the price of its existing products, the staff has to handle multiple customer queries regarding the hike. Lack of a satisfactory explanation would signify poor service standards and lead to customer dissatisfaction.

Reactive: A reactive approach basically consists of resorting to a predetermined service recovery mechanism once a customer complains about poor service quality. It usually starts with apologizing to the customer and then taking steps to redeem the situation. The fundamental flaw with this approach is that, here the customer has already had a bad experience of the brand's service.

Measuring Service Quality

Another crucial element to be kept in mind while seeking to maintain service quality is to have in place a metric for 'measuring' quality. The particular parameters selected would depend on the type of business, service model and the customer expectations. For example: at a customer service call center of a telecom provider, the metric for measuring service quality could be the average time taken for handling a call or rectifying a complaint. For a fast food outlet, the metrics for measuring service quality of the sales staff could be the number of bills generated as a percentage of total customer footfalls or the increase in sales month on month.

Once a system is put in place for measuring quality, a standard can then be mandated for the service standard the organization is seeking to maintain.

The Changing Face of Services Marketing

Marketing of Services has emerged as an important sub discipline of marketing in its own right. It has evolved phenomenally to emerge as a major field of study with far reaching implications in today's increasingly service driven economies. It is then, only natural, to wonder what is the future course that this field of study is most likely to take.

At first glance, one can see that there are as yet many opportunities available for Services Marketing to evolve and gain in relevance as the role of the service economy continues to expand. A large chunk of Third World economies are now beginning to move into the service domain. The role and share of the service sector in these economies is growing with an increased monetization of services

However, there are several challenges also. There has been a change in the basic nature of services. Services, today, can no longer be described according to the parameters of - intangibility, heterogeneity, inseparability and perishability. These changes are detailed below:

1. **Intangibility:** While services maybe intangible, the process of delivery and even the customer experience of the service is not necessarily so. Thus while service providers focus on pre purchase behavior they often fail to pay attention to customer experience during the process of service delivery, the nature of output (which may manifest in an observable physical change) or the learning outcomes of the delivery process.

2. **Heterogeneity:** Heterogeneity of services is also not applicable to the services domain today. Across sectors and industries we see an increased pressure for standardization of services. This is being achieved in some instances through automation such as through ATM's and vending machines. Even in cases where automation is not possible there is greater

focus on standardizing the service delivery process by way of service scripts and strict adherence to service cycles. For example, most fast food outlets and quick service restaurants follow the & steps of the service cycle that starts with greeting the customer (using standard phrases) through to saying good bye.

3. **Inseparability:** Even this criterion does not hold true for all services rendered. Inseparability implies that the production and consumption of services is simultaneous. Thus, consumers need to be present and/or involved in the production process. In reality however, there are several services that are separable. Example: insurance, repair and maintenance where production happens prior to consumption and the customers need not necessarily be present at the time the service is rendered. The same is witnessed in the phenomenon of outsourcing of services.

4. **Perishability:** even though this is true for a lot of services, there are several notable exceptions. In today's information era there are several information based services that can be recorded and saved in electronic media and reproduced on demand.

Moreover, for greater clarity in this regard it is necessary to have a distinction between the perishability of productive capacity, of customer experience and of the output.

Thus the definition of services is not as clear cut as it was once assumed to be. Consequently this is one of the major challenges lying ahead for the field of Services Marketing.

Service Industry at Cross Roads

No one would have ever imagined fifty years ago that the service sector would become a major contributor to the economy world over. Surprising but true, that in America as well as in India or in UK, service industry has grown beyond our imagination and continues to grow. Globalization and the advancement of technology has brought about a revolution in all of the service sectors be it hotel, airline or in software services. In fact service sector today employs the highest number of semi skilled and skilled manpower resources all over the world.

When you think of service, the picture that easily comes to your mind could be the McDonalds or Pizza-hut or the next best picture would be that of an airline. Our life has been made easier thanks to the service industry.

Customers are pampered with the best quality service making them demand more and more in terms of quality of services.

Services as we all know offers intangibles and can be qualified through the experience delivered to the customer. Service industry in the past few years has gone places. Automation and technology have helped standardize and bring in efficiency in service. **Service Organizations not only excel in offering timely and standardized service, they have gone one step ahead in offering personalized service to the customers too**. Today every customer is recognized individually by the hotel or the airline he visits. The hotel knows the customer's preferences and likes and are prepared to give him the best of customized service and engaging him in a relationship.

In a bid to offer the best of customized services and maintain the market share, service organizations have aggressively pursued various strategies internally. From Business process re-engineering, standard operating procedures, outsourcing and quality programs as well as all of the operational efficiency programs have been adopted and pursued aggressively in order to deliver faster and cheaper customer service performance. In the bargain to stay ahead of competition and increase their sales revenues, the companies have pursued marketing strategies more akin to that of product companies. The question that each of the companies have to ask themselves today is whether all of these have helped them become 'Market Leaders'. Companies may be operationally efficient and give the best service at the best price, but that hardly gives them the competitive edge over the others to lead the pack.

Take the case of Southwest airlines and Bank of America who have looked different from their competitors in their respective segments. Bank of America literally monopolized the American market with their fastest processing and delivery times for credit cards along with the best of customer service. South west airline managed to position themselves differently from the rest of the airlines in terms of value for money and no frills flying. While the rest of the competitors spent thousands of dollars in re-engineering processes and bringing in operational efficiencies to become profitable, this airline simply positioned itself differently.

What makes Southwest airlines as well as the other market leaders such as Wal-Mart, IKEA and Mc-Donald's is that they look at doing their business differently from the rest of the competition. When service offering is duplicated easily and every competitor is able to offer the same service at cheaper cost, it calls for service companies to think differently in order to retain their market leadership.

Leadership in Service Industry

The past few decades has seen unprecedented growth of service industry. In fact we can today say that the service industry is at its maturity stage. The gamut of services that make up for the significant contribution towards the GDP of the economy are numerous ranging from financial services, health care, hospitality, travel, insurance, information services, retail, utilities, information technology enabled services including social network and media services etc.

One of the prominent features of service industry that we see is the use of technology and standardized processes to drive operations. Every company makes investments into technology and offer gamut of services to the customers. Every service company tries its best to increase its operational efficiency and protect its bottom line while trying to increase its market share. Doing business efficiently and offering best service at the cheapest rates is what these companies are aiming to achieve. In the bargain most service organizations tend to lose out in the longer run and fail to see a real healthy growth in revenues. This happens only because they have failed to perceive the right direction and leadership strategies for service companies. Most often these companies are found to have adopted the strategies and plans that are appropriate for the 'Product' companies.

A service company needs to create that edge by doing things differently from the others, while continuing to strive for operational excellence and efficiency from within. While competition can easily duplicate the service offering, maintaining leadership calls for a different mindset and thinking in terms of continuous innovation and providing enhanced value of customer experience and service.

Southwest Airlines, McDonald's, Wal-Mart and credit card companies like Bank of America, Citi Bank credit cards have grown to become leaders in their market segment globally not only because of their service offerings and competitiveness, but by design to become customer centric Organizations that is driven to innovate all the time and outperform themselves all the time. The major different is that these organizations are built and think differently than the rest of the companies. These organizations too are driven by the same philosophy of operational efficiency, excellence and quality etc. But the difference lies not in their procedures but in the people that manage the operations and the management. Each of these Companies have tried to achieve excellence by choosing to focus few value propositions and create customized service experience that is difficult to be copied or matched by competition. When Bank of America introduced its credit cards in the market, they chose to build such robust processes and equipped with technology they promised fastest delivery of credit cards to the customers, which no other company could match at that point of time. The pain of having to apply and wait for the card to reach the customer through mail after due verification and authentication was something that this bank chose to attack and work to address this major pain point. While the rest of the credit card offerings would have been the same as the others in the market, they managed to score over the others and managed to establish their leadership overnight. This was not all, the company further went on to provide enhanced value to personalized customer service to customers. Any customer could expect the customer service to be flexible and go out of the way to facilitate the customer's special requests. The bank being a service industry had got their focus and strategy just right.

How to Maintain Competitive Edge in Service Industry

In the present times, doing business has become an extremely competitive game. This is true not only for the product industry but to the service industries as well. In case of service industry, the competition to be at the top and be the market leader is tougher simply because of the fact that service is all about intangibles unlike the product industry that sells a tangible product.

In a bid to grow and tap the market, the service companies in all sectors be it the hospitality, airlines or banks, all have been investing heavily into technology and bringing in standardization of service process and delivery operations. If you look at the marketing and sales channels adopted by the service industry, they tend to follow the same as product industry. Over a period of time, there is a very high chance that the service companies start looking at their business in the same way that the product companies do and the core service delivery part of their business might get sidelined.

When you go to a hotel, you are definitely taken in by the décor, their systems and procedures etc. However what makes you enjoy your stay and revisit the hotel or the restaurant has to do with your experience that you enjoy. A lot of other factors like the personal touch, quality of customized service, the attitude of the people serving as well as the efficiency and quality of service come into the picture. Therefore if the hotel s were to have the right processes and miss out on its personalized service aspect, it would fail to build customer loyalty, little realizing where it is going wrong.

Take the case of management consulting companies. No matter when tangible processes and tools they use to engineer their solutions, it is the consultants depth of experience and the knowledge that holds the key to the success of their solution. In such a case, if the company relies on its technology and tools to promote or market themselves, it does not attract the attention of a client who is looking for a solution.

What we are simply trying to say here is that, the service companies should realize that it is the core service intangibles that make the service offering and gives the service companies the competitive advantage and over a period of time, this point should not be lost sight of. The service continuum that is pursued by each of the service companies may be different. For example, two restaurants selling pizzas may pursue different service goals. One might focus on home delivery service and the other might focus on fastest delivery. The way that each company would need to pursue their respective core service goal would be different. The restaurant that wants to pursue the 'home delivery segment' would probably set up a separate order and delivery counters for home delivery. The packaging and the menu might be different for this section from that offered at the restaurant. The second company pursuing fastest delivery would put in place a time based order to delivery process and customize its menu as well as the delivery process to suit this goal.

Today all of the banks are heavily investing on technology and offering internet based services to the customers. So when the customers are able to use similar systems and obtain the same standard of services, which bank would they choose to bank with?. Obviously, the customers will look at the value addition that the bank is giving to its customers and choose to go with one whom he finds more beneficial. The value additions can come in the form of account management, expert advice, availability of umbrella products like investment options, insurance etc under one roof.

Banking sector in the current scenario gives us the perfect example to study how the service companies need to focus on their intangible services and not on the tangible service delivery systems to make a difference in the market.

Some Perspectives on Software Products versus Software Services

The Difference between Services and Products

The difference between services and products in software is that whereas the former involve work done for clients that are not the intellectual property of the vendor, the latter are patented by the vendor and sold

in terms of licenses to the users. Further, the difference between products and services in software is that whereas products usually represent high end work done by the vendors, services are usually middle to low end work that is done by the vendor. Apart from this, products entail higher value adding activities whereas services are lower value adding activities. Moreover, products need time and money to be invested to take them to fruition whereas services are usually measured in terms of the projects delivered within months or a year at the maximum. The key aspect about products and services in software is that products represent the culmination of several years of effort by the vendor who focuses on a specific niche to develop the products. On the other hand, services are usually projects that are done at the behest of the client and are billed according to time and material accounting or fixed cost accounting.

The Reason why the US is ahead and Asia lagging behind in Innovation

When we talk about software products and services, it needs to be mentioned that countries like the United States are ahead of the others in terms of innovation as the software and technology companies in the US make products instead of services. Think Microsoft or Apple and their game changing products. On the other hand, though countries like India are behemoths in the software industry, it is hard to find many companies that have developed products. Indeed, one of the reasons for outsourcing of services work from the West to the East is that the west can concentrate on higher value adding work like making products and by outsourcing the lower value adding work, they derive cost benefits as well as freeing up of resources that can be deployed for focusing on products. Further, the reason why the US is way ahead of the rest of the world in terms of innovation is that right from its inception, entrepreneurs were always on the lookout for game changing innovations and thus, when the software and technology industries and companies were being incubated, naturally the entrepreneurs in these sectors started to focus on products as a source of innovation.

Changing Trends in Products in Asia

However, some recent trends seem to suggest that Asian companies have realized the importance of software products as their software industries mature and hence, services become too low end to sustain them.

Further, now that they have significant capital reserves, they can deploy these resources in investing on product development. Remember that software products take a lot of investment of time and effort and hence, the Asian software industry is now finally realizing that as they have the needed capital as well as funding from venture capitalists from the west that sense an opportunity here, they can focus on building software products. Indeed, one of the best-known Asian companies that have a solid banking software product is Oracle Financial Services or the company that was previously known as i-Flex. This Indian company is a trailblazer as far as software products are concerned and because it invested a lot of time and money apart from effort in building the banking software product, it is now reaping the rewards of all that investment in terms of sales and reputation of its flagship product, Flexcube that is the largest selling banking software product in the world.

Concluding Remarks

Now that we have discussed how products and services square up against each other, it would be worthwhile to note that not all companies can afford to build software products because of the reasons mentioned in the previous sections. Therefore, the role of venture capitalists and angel investors is especially crucial in this respect.

Getting Ahead of the Race in Service Industry

Service industry today dominates the economic scene in all the countries. Over a period of few decades we have seen the rise and unprecedented growth of service industry in almost all sectors including technology and telecommunications, health care, education, media, Utilities, financial and banking sector etc.

Service industries growth has been characterized by focusing on customer service which hereto pushed the product companies too to reorient themselves to look at the customers first. The concept of 'Customer Is The King' has come about thanks to the Service industry. In the next cycle, we see service companies having embraced technology and used technology to upgrade their service offerings altogether. This is true in all of the service sectors including the traditional hospitality and travel industries as well. Technology not only helped the service industries to scale up their business operations, it helped bring about standardization in the operations and service delivery mechanisms. At this point we see service industries beginning to align themselves to product industry culture of standardizing operations and processes and embracing the same principles of operational efficiency, quality of service and other concepts. They have also borrowed the concepts of process re-engineering and other costing methods to manage their business operations.

Today we believe that the service industry is in a mature stage. Competition in Service industry is tougher than the product industry simply because one is dealing with intangible services and customer experience as well as perceptions which can be highly subjective. What we see is that all of the service industry players in all segments have been using technology and standardized processes as enablers of their business. In the rat race, there is every chance that the service company loses its focus on the service experience as one of its deliverables and gets busy in pursuit of revenue targets and market share. This danger of forgetting that one is in the business of delivery customer delight and satisfaction in terms of experience may be lost sight of.

When all of the companies given similar scale of operations are following the same standard

procedures and similar systems to manage their business, how does one become a market leader?. The answer to this question lies in 'doing things differently'. Take a look at the airline sector for example. When the competition is so stiff, two companies have thrived amidst tough competition. South West and Virgin Atlantic have managed to become leaders by innovating themselves differently from that of competition. Southwest grabbed attention with its no frills flying and offering the cheapest airfares, while Virgin Atlantic has built not only a business but a brand successfully. If you read the Virgin Atlantic case study, you will realize that the airline has invented many 'Firsts' in customer service by offering a brand new in-flight experience with entertainment as well as in flight services including personalized services such as foot massage, customized meals etc in flight. They have followed this up with specialized origin and destination services offering company chauffeur driven car from the airport including special services such as 'drive in check in' at certain airports. According to Richard Branson - "A brand name that is known internationally for innovation, quality and a sense of fun is what we have always aspired to with Virgin."

Those companies that realize the value of their core service offering and focus continually on innovating their service offering and ensuring increased customer benefit and value will naturally find themselves ahead of the game in the long run.

What is Social Media Marketing ? - Meaning and Important Concepts

We Humans are essentially social animals. Communication and interaction is vital for the Human society. People love to socialize and interact with one another. Internet technology has changed the way the people communicate. Gone are the days when one had to write a letter or book a telephone call to speak to a friend or relative living across the country. Today technology enables one to be in touch with friends and family across the globe instantaneously.

Look at any individual's lifestyle today. Most often you will find people spending over two to three hours every evening on the internet chatting with friends and communicating with likeminded people. People of all ages tend to find social networking sites that deal with the subject of their interest and follow the conversations happening there. Internet being a global phenomenon, you will find people from all over the world coming together to talk and share information about their particular topic of interest. It had never been easier that this to make friends and socializing over the internet.

When we talk of social networking we are not just referring to the chatting and other blogs and forums where people discuss certain topics. We seem to be using the social media for sharing videos, movies, music, photos and all of the information that one would want to share. Millions of viewers log into You Tube to view the latest movies, clippings etc. every minute. Similarly millions are logging into face book searching for friends online and sharing information about self with friends all the time. Flickr happens to be the most favorite site for photo sharing.

When you want to know the definition or meaning of a particular word or a topic, what do you do?. It is quite likely that you will check out the Wikipedia or Encyclopedia sites online. If you follow the history of Wikipedia, it best describes the growth and power of social media. Wikipedia is a site that allows anyone and everyone to contribute topics, explanations and definitions at its site. The information so provided can be reviewed by those interested and anybody can comment or provide corrections as well as further explanations. Thus the topics are built, reviewed, changed and reformed through the collective effort of people who are interested in the particular topic. This is perhaps the best example of social media network where people come together to discuss, deliberate, communicate and create content that is useful to one and all.

When you look at the social media marketing websites from the eyes of the marketing companies, one gets to see a huge potential waiting to be explored. Social media networks represent markets and customers who are online and listening. With captive audience being available, marketing companies can reach out to the prospective customers and help build opinion about their products and services as well as initiate discussion about their products with the help of those who are interested as well as those who have been customers of the company. Marketers can learn a lot and get real feedback about their product and experiences from the customers online and besides initiate interest in others who are watching and following the topic.

Social media marketing is a phenomenon and this is a medium that no marketing Organization can afford to ignore or be absent from.

Social Media Characteristic Aspects

Internet has changed people's lifestyle as well as habits. Primarily every human being has a need and wish to communicate with others and exchange information, ideas, news etc. Internet has enabled people to connect and communicate with not only one's family, but with people across the world. Truly internet has erased the boundaries between nations.

The participation from community of people and society at large has provided impetus to the growth of Social Media Network. There is hardly anybody who is not participating in one or the other type of social media, be it exchanging emails, using chat or posting photographs and exchanging music etc.

With the increasing number of online community participation, the social media network has become a major medium that is being explored by Marketers, who find it the most effective way of getting closer to the customers and getting to know the customers. Marketers have dual advantage in the fact that they are able to get in touch with those who have already become their customers and experienced their products as well as those prospective customers who might be inclined to or may be influenced to buy the product.

Features

Social media when compared to traditional news media is different in several fundamental aspects.

Unlike the traditional media where the readers or viewers are passive participants, social media network is one place where the customers as well as 'would be' customers are actively participating and exchanging information, sharing experience, giving their opinion and reviews based on their understanding as well as experience. This means that the markets are able to interact with the customer in 'real time' basis and benefit from the communication. The Organization actually gets to 'listen' to the customer and understand more about the customer's perception about the brand as well as the product etc. The social media channels help build collective opinion and precipitate healthy discussions about the relevant topics.

Second important feature is that social media network spread across variety of channels and medium as compared to the limited channels that print and news media operate with. Social media network operates with several tools including audio, video, text, audio pods, and private forums, public discussion boards, SMS, chatting, emails as well as blogging etc.

Thirdly, social media network is a dynamic, flexible medium that keeps changing interms of content, tools and keeps evolving all the time. As the participants keep giving inputs and the collective wisdom of the group results in change and up-dation of the content as well as creates demand for more tools to be made available.

Fourthly, social media network calls for a different kind of participation from the marketers. Unlike the traditional media where marketers run campaigns and customer designed advertisements focused on a particular audience or group, social media network enables the participants to steer the discussion and the marketers are required to do more of listening than leading the discussion. Marketers have got to approach the prospective customers in a indirect fashion by helping to build public opinion and then indirectly steer them towards taking an interest in your product.

Social media network is evolving at a very fast pace and in line with faster changing technology tools that are being made available. Marketers have got no option but to tune in with the media, understand how things work and make sure they are present. Not being present in the social media networks in the current times is not an option for marketing companies.

Insight into Social Media Networks from Marketers Point of View

Spending a few hours every evening blogging or chatting with friends across the world or uploading photos and commenting , have become a way of life for millions of people. Social Media has enabled large community of people to communicate and interact with one another like never before. Social Media provides free access to individuals to read, write, share information, contribute their view point, participate in discussions, share photos, music, videos, and build collective opinions and discussions around a common topic of interest besides of course enabling people to make friends. The possibilities for social interactions are unlimited.

As far as the marketers are concerned, social media is a huge world of opportunities where one is able to directly reach out and interact with prospective customers as well as existing customers. Today Companies have no option but to be in the social media by compulsion rather than by choice.

The fact that the social media contributions and discussions are held by the community of people, they have the freedom to discuss about any company, any product and influence the opinion of the others. Therefore it becomes important for marketers to be in tune with the communities on the social media and to listen to them. It is only by listening to the customers and their opinions as well as experiences about your products that the marketers are able to get a real feedback on the product performance and take suitable actions based on the feedback. Marketers should also realize that by tuning in with the participants in the social web, one is not only able to listen and thus get the pulse of the public; it gives the markets a strategic approach on how to influence and approach the prospective customers in the given circumstances.

Marketers have got to understand the fundamental differences between other marketing channels and social media networks. **Social media networks are the most direct channel that provides access to the 'would be' customers and existing customers.** However it is also important to note that the conversations and information between the communities and individuals on various forums and blogs is totally voluntary or collaborative. Unlike in the other media channels where marketers are able to target the audience through direct advertisements or mails and other forms of advertisements, on the social web media, marketers have no absolute control over the discussions and at best can influence the communities by participating and guiding the discussions around its products and information.

Another aspect of social media networks that is of importance to the marketers is that the medium provides the real and instant feedback from the actual users about the products and services. One may wonder if the feedback and the opinions expressed are genuine and if the total feedback is accurate. The fact that the process of collective opinion evolving out of discussions over a period of time can vary, can mean that the representation of the opinions and overall feedback can also vary over a period of time. Further it can be subject to the influences from the marketer's side and thus at the end the opinions might change altogether from what it was in the first place. Since the feedback is received from genuine customers who have the real experience, it has been seen over a period of time that the opinions and feedback is generally very accurate and the marketers can bank on the same. In several cases, one can also measure the feedback using various tracking and surveying tools.

End of it, marketers need to realize the fact that **social media networks work as an extension of the other major media channels through which the Companies target the customers**. Marketers cannot rely only on social media networks to target their media campaigns to the customer groups. At the same time, they cannot help but be present in the social media networks, for as long as the competition is present in the social media and as long as the people are discussing about the Product and the Company, one has no choice but to participate in the social media process.

How is Social Media Different from Other Media

Social Media Network and the different channels have caught on the fancy of young and adults alike and this phenomenon has spread all over the globe. Every minute there are thousands of people logging into the internet and engaging in conversation using one or the other channels of online communication. Similarly there are millions of users of social media network in one form or the other. To a marketing professional or company, this can only mean one thing, that even if half of them were to be interested in their product, they have a huge business opportunity on hand.

It is often seen that more than sixty percent of the individuals are engaging in conversation about one or the other product, service and sharing their knowledge as well as experience. Thus the collective opinion or the word of mouth publicity and opinion generated has such dynamic potential that no Company can afford to ignore. Whether a Company wishes to or not, they have no option but to be present and participate in the Social Media Network today.

For Management students and Marketing professions, it is very essential to understand all about this medium in detail. **Understanding of the evolution of Social Media Network as it is today is essential for it gives one an in-depth understanding of media effect as well as consumer behavior**.

Internet began to become popular in the 1980s when computers began to become affordable and the penetration of computers into homes and personal use as well as business use began to increase exponentially. Advancement of technology gave way to higher bandwidth and speed in internet leading to broadband and Wi-Fi connections. Before internet became popular, it was the normal habit of individuals across the world to be glued to TV and reading Newspapers. Marketing and media industry had been used to targeting audience and designing campaigns as well as advertisements for print media and using the commercial break slots in the TV programs for airing their advertisements. At this stage the audience though they did not like it, had no choice but to watch the advertisements for they were not in control of the medium.

With the advent of internet and introduction of emails, the meaning of communication and advertising changed all together. When some of the people from internet industry experimented using commercial content in emails, they realized that they had a huge opportunity on hand. At the click of a button, and in a inexpensive way they could now access and target millions of audience by sending advertisements and marketing communication through emails. Quickly this trend in the industry caught on and resulted in a new industry running spam mails.

Though the individuals did not have any control over the TV advertisements, the spam mails was not something that they enjoyed receiving, especially because it was unsolicited and secondly it was directed to them in person and dropping into their personal inbox without their permission. A public outcry and sustained reservation against spamming resulted in the birth of anti spamming tools, programs and companies specializing in anti spamming lawsuits.

Parallel to the email spamming we also witnessed the birth of online advertising on the websites which did not intrude upon any individual's privacy by sending unsolicited emails but provided advertising banners and tags on which one could click and get directed to the particular website of the company selling the product etc.

There have been several developments in online advertising on the internet.

The development of Social Media Network at this juncture has been a very positive and welcome change that has been accepted widely by the users across the globe. This has become popular simply because the control over the discussions and content remains essentially with the users and not the company's advertising or participating. Secondly the discussions take place in the form of simple conversations and collective participation of people by choice. Everyone is able to express their opinions.

The fact that Social Media is participative and the power lies with the audience and not with the advertisers or the marketing companies is something that the marketing professionals have got to understand, for such an understanding will give them the direction for building their online marketing as well as online advertising strategy besides guiding them on how to participate and influence the audience on the Social Web.

Understanding Social Web from Marketing Viewpoint

If you sit back and look at the kind of traffic that is going through the Internet, you might be surprised. At any given point of time millions of people are exchanging messages, chatting and conversing with one another. We might very well assume that the percentage of people using the various social network channels to communicate with one another would be much larger that the online trading and other commercial transactions taking place.

Logging into internet and chatting, downloading movies, music, reading reviews, participating in discussions, listening to podcasts and SMS etc have become a part of the lifestyle of every household across the world. This is true in case of retired persons, housewives, and working professionals to children of all ages. Everybody is able to find something relevant and useful in the social web.

When millions are talking to one another, they are essentially talking about a particular topic of interest or sharing their experiences etc. Such conversations generate a lot of word to mouth publicity to various products and services that the individuals are talking about. Thus the marketers find it a great opportunity to harvest the social web for potential customers who are interested in their products.

To be able to use the social web as an effective marketing tool, the marketing professionals have got to understand all about the social web and how it works. Social web works differently from other forms of media including visual media. Social web networks are largely driven by content that is produced by the collective community that engages in conversation. Such conversations build opinions and influence the decisions of the prospective customers. Reviews, Discussions, ratings and comments etc provide measurable feedback from the customers who have experienced the products and services that they are referring to.

At this juncture it is important for the Marketers to remember that the social web channels are controlled not by them but by the participants. The two main characteristic features of this medium where in people engage in conversation are that it gives rise to word of mouth publicity or opinion and an element of trust exists between the individuals and communities that are engaging in discussions. Taking the above into account, the marketers have got to come up with strategy of how to influence the opinions and make way for positive experience for the prospective customers.

If you analyze the composition of the participants engaging in discussions in the social web, there are principally two categories of people. First is the category that has already purchased, used and experienced your product or service and the second category belongs to those who have not purchased or used and this category includes prospective customers who are participating in the discussions only because they are interested in considering to make a purchase at a future point of time. Therefore the social media becomes a channel that connects those who have experienced the product to those that are waiting to experience the product. If this concept is clearly understood by the marketing personnel, they would be able to devise ways of harnessing the social web as a medium for influencing and selling to the prospective customers successfully. A marketing manager should be able to first identify the buying process and map it clearly to be able to get into the field of social web and build prospective sales conversion channel out of the prospective customer base.

Approach to Learning about Social Web for Marketing Professionals

If internet has affected the lives of millions of people across the world and brought them together through social media networks, the same technology and tools have reinvented the marketing and media campaign strategies for the marketing companies too. No big time business can ignore the social web today. By virtue of the fact that the individuals present and participating in the social web are talking about the product or services relevant to each one's business, the companies have got to be present to be able to address the prospective buyers who are also present and are listening to the reviews, comments, ratings and feedback of those who have purchased and use the products.

Every Marketing professional would need to include the social media into his marketing campaign and integrate the same with the rest of the media channels that he is currently using. The starting point of this journey would be to understand the technology, the platform, the various channels and all about how social web works. Secondly one needs to understand and watch what happens on the social web when individuals and groups are talking to one another across the network. Understanding of the behavior of the participants across the social web channels is very important for it is this audience that the marketing companies are concerned about and it is this group of people that consist of the existing customers and would be customers of the company.

Social media has been used effectively by all kinds of businesses including the Hollywood movies for their premier releases to the Home Store Depots. Social web channels like SMS, Youtube and Facebook etc have been harnessed effectively for building instant awareness about the product or service. Thus marketers have realized the huge potential that exists in being able to reach out to a large customer base at negligible cost. Understanding of this aspect of the consumer behavior on the social web is a must for any marketing professional wishing to design social media campaign for his company. The awareness factor can be positive or result in negative publicity too. Therefore one needs to be able to influence if not directly control the audience reaction through well designed and orchestrated participation in the events and discussions on the web.

One other factor that stands out amongst the users and participants of social media is the element of trust. Those who are discussing and are participating in the discussions implicitly trust the words of all the others who ever is involved. Therefore when a Company is participating in the discussions and influencing the discussion, it is assumed by one and all that what is being said is true one hundred percent. Therefore it becomes important on the part of the Organization to ensure that what is being said is true and that it delivers what it promises. One must always remember that the existing customers would make up their mind about the product or service depending upon the extent and level of satisfaction derived out of the product or service in relation to their expectation from such product or service. Thus **it is important for the Marketing professional to first understand how the social web audience's discussions works as an effective feedback to the prospective customers and builds their awareness as well as influences their decision to purchase**. Secondly there is a need to be able to synchronize the media campaign on the social web with the operations so that whatever is committed is delivered.

Understanding Group Behaviour on Social Web

Internet has given way to new means of communication and interaction between people situated across the globe, breaking down the barriers of distance, time and borders. Technology has made it possible for people not only to talk to one another, but participate in a lot of activities together as a group. Thus **group activities or the so called networks in the language of social web media are growing and discovering the concept of collective wisdom as an outcome of group discussions on any subject**. Social web consists of several channels including Blogs, Forums, Photo/Video Sharing, Music sharing, Emails, Chatting, SMS, Podcasting, Micro blogs and wikis etc. Facebook, Youtube, Linkedin, Farmville, Wikipedia etc are some of the best known faces of social web.

For anyone in marketing, social web is something that he or she needs to understand not only as a participant but more importantly as a marketing professional representing his or her Organization. The social web and the networks of people consists of the existing customers and the prospective customers who would be exchanging information, discussing their experiences as consumers and thus helping the prospective customers build their awareness as well as influence their purchasing decisions.

When it comes to understanding the behavior of the participants and groups involved in any of the social media channels, one must first visit the various channels to see the kind of network that exists. In some of the channels, you will find individuals talking to other individuals and chatting. There exist discussions amongst group members regarding one common topic under blogs and forums. You will also find inter group discussions and one group talking to another and debating about issues and topics too. All of these groups and networks command power to influence the outcome of the discussions and the opinions. Therefore understanding the group dynamics and identifying the controlling, influencing as well as moderating elements and factors would come in handy while designing strategy to participate and influence the discussions from the point of view of marketing.

One Of the most important and powerful aspect of the discussions amongst the groups and in between the groups is that they are able to build intelligent arguments and factual content by filtering, wetting and helping others make informed choice as well as strengthening the consumer's bargaining power. The fact that it is easy to gather all information just by asking questions and being able to understand everything about a product that there is to know about and having access to those who have used the product and others who are able to throw light and help with right decision making is what makes people flock to the social web with their needs and requirements. Individuals find it worthwhile to discuss and gather information about the products and services they are interested in and at the same time enjoy socializing in a manner of speaking.

Marketers would do well to remember that when it comes to Social Web, it is not what the Marketer chooses to advertise and inform the customers that matters, but it is the actual experience and opinion of the customers who are participating in the social media networks and discussing with the others that matters. As a marketer one has the power to influence the discussion and how well one can win the trust and confidence of the group depends upon the strategy and implementation of the communication plan. This in turn calls for a complete hands on understanding of and presence in the social web all the time as well as being able to read the pulse of the group at all times.

Understanding Social Media Channels

As Marketing professional or a management professional, one needs to be in tune with the current trends, especially in terms of the media channels and be ahead of the customers. Social Media networking has brought about phenomenal changes to the consumer behavior. While traditionally print media, Audio and Video media were one sided communication channels providing information through advertisement to the readers and viewers with or without their approval, the social media channels on the other hand are interactive and controlled by the consumers themselves.

Advertising to the prospective customers in current times involves using multiple mediums including print, TV, Websites, Blogs, You Tube, Facebook, Flickr and onsite etc. Marketing Companies today have no option but to be available in all leading channels. Therefore drawing up a communication and advertising strategy calls for designing a separate social media strategy after understanding all about Social Media Networks, the Consumer Behavior, the Characteristics and importantly the different elements.

Some of the most popular channels of social web happen to be the blogs, social networks, photo-sharing sites, audio (Pod Cast) and video sharing, Wikis, Email, SMS and micro-blogging etc. In this section we shall briefly discuss blogs and wikis which happen to be very popular medium of conversation on the web.

Blogs

A blog is a webpage where people post comments, reviews or write about a given topic and share information. Bloggers first started writing blogs as single author pages and the viewers would then start commenting and the discussions would ensue in the form of posts. However in recent times, the professional blogging has come of age where multiple authors write and contribute to the blogs on various subjects and topics. You can find blogs in almost all fields including personal, professional, business related, academic and research etc. In fact the blogs from Universities, Research and interest based groups in on the increase. Unlike earlier where blogs were maintained by individuals, the trend now has shifted to blogs being written by multiple authors enhancing the content as well as quality of discussions.

Until a few years ago, the blogs used to contain text messages or posts. In current times the professional blogs contain video, audio and image clippings etc. making it an enriching experience for viewers. Marketing companies use such blogs for online brand building and advertising. The fact that the world wide web contains more than 175 million blogs speaks for its popularity as a channel.

Every marketing manager and management student would need to take time to go through various types of blogs and understand all about them. One should be able to identify the theme of the blog, estimate the volume of posts, see the pattern of comments and the posts and be able to feel the pulse of the individuals. Understanding the tone and the way in which discussions are held and moderated will give one an idea of how to use this channel effectively for online marketing.

Terminology & Resources

The blogging community is referred to by the trade as 'Blogsphere'. Similar to websites, the blogs too contain link backs, blog rolls and other features that enable the various blogs to be interconnected and network with one another.

To search for blogs on various topics, several blog search engines are available namely Technorati, Blog Scope etc. They provide search options to look for the recent and popular tags used in blog postings etc. Online community of bloggers namely Blog Catalog, Global Voices and many more sites provide connections to multiple bloggers and groups too.

Several marketing companies and businesses create and maintain their own blogs created solely for the purpose of promoting their products and advertising for the same. Such companies engage the services of professional bloggers to create post content in line with the social media strategy design given by the Company.

Social Web Channels and Features - RSS Feeders

Millions of people all over the world have been discovering the pleasure of logging into the internet and connecting with friends from all over the world. Hours are spent blogging, chatting or SMSing as well as sharing photos, videos etc. People are discovering the power of communication and community discussions on blogs. No wonder the number of blogs on the internet is increasing by the day and has crossed over 175 million. This phenomenon is not going to slow down anytime soon.

Using internet to search for information on various websites as well as checking out the blogs and asking questions to know all about any topic or product of interest has become the most common way for people to gather information. When it comes to any business area, the social web consists of participants who have been customers and are able to offer their opinion and experience to the 'would be' prospective customers. Therefore the social web becomes important for every Business Organization for this is where their customers are listening and discussing, to make up their mind to go ahead with the purchase they intend to make.

Marketing Managers and other media persons have got to have a detailed understanding of how Social Media Networks work and are evolving. They need to know the pulse of the bloggers and other users of internet channels to be able to build an effective communication strategy on social web. Social Media Network consists of several channels including blogs, forums, wikis, podcasts, audio, video and photo sharing as well as SMS and chatting, Emails etc.

In this section we shall briefly cover an introduction to RSS.

RSS stands for 'Really Simple Syndication'. Every time you see any executive checking his blackberry or a lady checking out her smartphone, you should know that they are reading the RSS update that they have received recently.

Normally those who browse the net will have interest in various areas and visit several websites regularly. Some websites may not be viewed daily and one would wish to go to the website to check out any new content or updates only. Earlier on the websites had begun to send an email update to the subscribers intimating them of the news update on the website and providing a link to the website. However now everybody uses the RSS feeder which works faster and is simpler. RSS is a feeder and information program that sends the updates, headlines and very small messages to the subscribers. As people are in the habit of following news, political updates, weather, sports, movies as well as some of the favorite stars and many subject oriented websites, blogs etc., it helps them to subscribe to RSS feeds from each of these website and receive update alerts on to their smart phones and computers. Thus it saves them from the effort and time of having to check out each of the websites for new content. Check out any of the latest websites including BBC, CNN etc and you will find a feature called 'RSS Subscribe' inviting you to subscribe to the RSS notifications on that particular website.

Following are some of the popular RSS Feed icons:

RSS Aggregators

RSS aggregator programs go one step further to syndicate all the RSS that one is interested in and subscribes to and provides the new content updates from amongst the RSS list that has been fed into the aggregator or RSS Reader software. By subscribing to RSS Aggregator, the viewers gets to save a lot of time having to go through each of the RSS updates and gets to view only the updated RSS feed and thereby access the particular website.

How Does Marketing Company Benefit by Using RSS Feed ?

RSS Feeds can be used to intimate the customers as well as the prospective buyers about any updates on product, services, introduction of new brands, technology or any update relating to the Company, business or products and services etc. This can be the fastest way of reaching the customers and getting their attention. News of any discount sale announced or schemes announced can be circulated to thousands of customers using RSS feed in a matter of few minutes.

Social Networks - A Key Element of the Social Web

Any Company marketing its products and services cannot afford to ignore or keep away from the Social Networks and Social Web. The fact that people on the social networks are talking and sharing information about products and services makes it imperative for Companies to participate. Social Networks are great platforms for individuals to participate and converse freely with others of similar interest. **Social networks consist of individuals as well as communities that have common interest. This is an important interest group as far as marketers are concerned.** Though they may not be addressing the entire mass at a given time like they do through traditional media, here the participants make up for specific community of people as well as individuals. When individuals are conversing with one another, sharing their likes, dislikes as well as their experiences, they are not only talking about their life's experiences, but a significant part of what ever they have purchased, reviewed, seen or experienced in terms of product and services also form a part of the discussion. If they are discussing about a certain product or service, then it becomes important for that particular Company to be listening as well as participating in order to add to the discussion, to clarify or to substantiate its stand etc. To be able to develop communication strategy for Social Web, it is important to understand all of the components, tools as well as the various networks and the participants in particular. Understanding of the participant's expectations, behavior as well as requirements gives one a clue as to how to communicate with the audience.

One of the key aspects of understanding the various elements of the Social Web would be to understand and go through the various Social Networks. **Social Networks form a part of the Social Web and refer to**

communities and platforms that interact with several other communities and groups and thus interact over a wider social network. Individuals who frequent Social Networks do not limit themselves to being a part of any one or two communities. They like to be a part of wider network and subscribe to several networks of interest. Social web consists of several types of networks. Most importantly you have the communities that exist purely for the purpose of socializing and entertainment while you also have the communities that are specific to business or certain profession etc. It would be very useful for all to review Facebook as well as Myspace and Twitter, the leading Social networks and study them. There are several country specific social networks that are popular and accordingly it would be apt to choose the local social networking sites too as a part of study along with few of the global networking sites. You will be able to see the variety and depth of information that they provide to the members as well as the wide coverage of subscriber base that they enjoy. It is important to understand the service offering as well as the volume of traffic, the pulse of the participants as well as have a look at how business communities are targeting the members on these Social Networks.

Apart from the above Social Networks, it is important to visit few of the business related Social Networks like Linkedin, Plaxo Plus etc would be the most important ones that can provide substantial information about how the communities network and function. It makes sense to study these in detail and see how the other businesses are targeting the audience on these sites, what kind of communication style is being adapted etc.

End of the study, one should be able to differentiate between Social sites and Business Sites, understand the difference between the communities and participants and be able to identify the strategy ideal to advertise or market to each of these communities.

Advertising on Social Networks

Marketing has always been relying on traditional print and visual media for advertising their products and services. The basis of the mass media both in print as well as in visual form is to release one common advertisement to the entire mass in general. Such advertising is controlled by the marketers who have control over the release of the advertisement and the audience or the readers and viewers have very little control viewing or watching such advertisements. It is a very well known fact that most people do not enjoy the interruptions on the TV shows and the commercial breaks that beam advertisements.

The fact is that the audience does not have a say in the matter. The only choice people have and which they often exercise is to take a break, skip the commercial break and resume watching TV when their show starts back.

With the arrival of internet and social web, the concept of advertising online and through the social networks has taken a different turn.

In the beginning when marketers discovered that they could send emails and messages to the mass at fraction of cost, there began a boom with everyone sending unwanted messages to all the email IDs that they could get hold of. This has tapered off to a large extent due to the hit back from the recipients who find the messages irrelevant and an invasion into their privacy. With the next wave came the advertisements in the form of banners and sponsored links and displays on web pages. One can click on these banners and flashers and get directed to the relevant page of the Company.

Advertising on Social Network is a different ball game. The network consists of communities of people who are discussing, sharing and conversing with one another and building opinions in the process. Therefore the advertisers and marketers do not have control. **The advertising on the social network functions like traditional channels as well as in the form of non-interruptive advertising**. Advertisements that pop up on web pages, the banners work like traditional channels and are interruptive, whereas the new kind of advertising and marketing known as Embedded Marketing Application has introduced non-interruptive as well as interactive advertising.

The best example that one can see in terms of Embedded Marketing Application is the application called Product Pulse on Face book. The application engages the audience with new products and services by inviting them to rate the product as per their opinion and invites them to join some of the easy to win contests too. This aspect makes a lot of sense for marketers as it gives a lot of information about the consumer behavior as well as the pulse of the consumer.

Understanding and viewing the social networks as well as business networks on the internet can give one an idea of what is the effective way of communicating with people on the networks and how to manage the expectations as well as to engage the customer from advertising and selling point of view.

Brand Building, Launch and Promotion on Social Web

Social Networks provide great opportunity for advertising as well as promoting the brands. The fact that you can present your brand in front of over 200 million people who are participating in the discussions at various Social Networks provides a different dimension to the concept of advertising.

It is important for us to remember that Social Networks are essentially different from traditional media channels. While **traditional media channels are purely one way communication channels where the viewers have no choice, the Social Networks on the other hand provide for consumer participation, active discussion**

and thus promotes the building of the reputation of the brand.

Social Networks thrive on connections with others, discussions as well as conversations about experiences of the people and provide platform for expression of opinions and reviews. This process of how the reputation and opinions are formed on the Social networks holds the key to building a successful brand promotional strategy on the social web.

While the bigger brands and proven brands may be present in the same platform, there is sufficient scope for a new emerging brand to make its mark and create a buzz amongst the viewers, which then is likely to spread across the networks and thus help grow the brand reputation. Understanding of the communication process and human psychology would help in positioning a product or brand in the social web.

One of the major noticeable characteristics of the Social Networks is that people often make their comments and give opinions based on their experiences. The normal conversation tends to be centered about what one did or experienced. For example, if the topic of the conversation happens to be the

Wimbledon matches, it is quite likely that people who have been travelling to the place are likely to talk about the weather as well as the hotels. They are likely to provide real and authentic feedback about their stay. When the hotel becomes the topic of conversation, the others would also join in and share their experiences as well as comments thus forming a collective opinion. If the particular hotel were to be present and contributing to the conversation, it is likely that they can help influence the discussion and help gain good brand publicity or reputation. The fact that the hotel is present and is able to participate officially lends credibility and the participants will accept whatever is presented by the Hotel as authentic and official. Thus the interaction between the participants and the hotel can help build loyalty and a good reputation amongst the community. Further on, the same sentiments are likely to get dispersed to other communities as well.

When Companies wish to introduce a new brand into the market. Social network provides the right platform for launching the same. In fact Companies are known to engage with consumers over social networks for a long time before the planned launch and build an online community around the same. Thus they are able to present their plan, understand and evaluate the reactions of the consumers which gives them a huge insight into the psyche of the market and understand the consumers better. If used intelligently such online communities that have been created around the specific brand can be used as a launch vehicle which will help the marketing and advertising immensely during the actual launch.

Advertisement Planning on Social Web

Internet age and the social web is redefining marketing. Online marketing as well as online advertising and brand promotions are done differently from the traditional ways. When you consider the traditional way of marketing and building customer loyalty, you will find that the customer's positive experience of the product or service helps build loyalty. **It is interesting to study the same aspect on Social Networks to identify and establish the way in which the online community builds and endorses a product or service.**

Online interactions on the social networks are carried out by individuals and at the same time the opinions and the loyalty expressed would be collective. This is not so in the case of traditional media. Another significant factor to be noted is that the online community participant's subscribership can be measured and quantified. The entire process of loyalty building can be easily tracked and traced on social web. On the Social Networks, one may not necessarily speak about loyalty to the brand, but the same concept is referred to as the reputation of a brand.

The brand reputation is built as a result of the conversations and discussions held by individuals but the reputation is built by the participation and collective opinion of the entire community. Further on the community opinion helps strengthen the individual participant's loyalty or commitment towards the brand. The reputation build by a community is further harnessed and spread to other networks and slowly a buzz begins to form around the brand. The new launches of products ride on such buzz and gain popularity across millions of subscribers.

At this point, it is important for the marketers to map and understand the behavior as well as the attributes of the individual participants as well as the community as a whole. By understanding both, the collective as well as the individual, it is possible to influence one to impact the other. Thus the Company can work to influence the community in which case the individual too gets influenced automatically.

Every marketer would need to know the basic difference between traditional media channels and the social web. **On the Social web, the advertising or marketing is not unilateral but is participative. It is the participants who control the Social Web and discussions and not the Company alone**. One might think of not being present on the Social Web. But thinking in this way can be a big mistake. If the customers are available in the form of online community and if they are discussing your product or service, it is important for you to be participating too. Absence from the Social web in such situations can cause damage to the Company's reputation which might be viewed adversely by the collective community.

Social web alone cannot be the complete solution for marketing or advertising products and services to the markets. The Social Web would have to be used as supplementary to the traditional channels. If you understand the trend amongst the people, you will find that every individual tends to check out the details of products or services that he gets to see on the TV or print media. This goes on to prove the need for marketing on Social Web.

Who Controls the Social Web Content? - Marketers Don't

Those who are avid bloggers spend hours on internet discussing and sharing information with others over several social networks. Blogging, Chatting and streaming music as well as videos and making new friends as well as checking out new sites and networks is how most people spend their evenings with. Social web has enabled the users to use several multi-media tools and thus given them the freedom to express themselves through any of the written, audio or video mediums. Communication and social interaction is one of the basic tendencies of human beings and society at large. Over the web, people tend to share their experiences, views and all about what is happening in their life as well as around them. Therefore be it information about their travel experience or the anniversary and birthday celebrations, you will find individuals discussing several issues. Featured in their discussion will be the reference to various products or services that they have come across or used. Their experience in use of or their knowledge and awareness of the product as well as their perceptions get to be known and discussed widely.

When a group discussion takes place regarding any product or service, the response can be positive or negative depending upon the members and the trend of the discussion. A marketer would definitely be interested in this niche segment to ensure that he contributes to the discussions and helps build brand loyalty. Content on Social networks is largely built or created by the individual participants. Every individual is capable of creating and uploading any content that he feels is right. The experts in the Social Web consultancy call this as Consumer generated media and includes all kinds of blogs, videos, photos, music as well as reviews, ratings etc. **Marketers would do well to remember that all of the content is generated by the participants and they control the way the discussions are developed and opinions are formed**.

If the Marketers are not able to control the content and discussions on social networks, how can they participate and get their message across the audience?. Understanding and measuring the blogs and other networks helps the marketers design the strategy to participate and market their products and services online and influence the social networks. Measurement and tagging of blogs provides detailed information to the Marketers about the number of forums, the number of participants as well as the general trend of opinion regarding their product or service category. As people discuss anything and everything connected to their life and experiences, a lot of data be it regarding price of an airline ticket, the stay at a hotel or about discounts offered on automobiles and shopping experiences surface in the discussions. **Understanding and analyzing the feedback received from such social networks can be used effectively by the Organization to fine tune their product or service offering as well as create niche products or services for each segment**. Using the same multimedia tools in terms of audiovisuals etc, you can demonstrate the product performance, features or an experience which will be far more effective than just words. When the feedback gets translated into action and the same is intimated by the marketer to the participants in the network, the customers are likely to appreciate such response and the brand loyalty or the reputation is likely to grow.

To be successful on the Social Web, the marketer has got to be present and actively participating with the related groups. Though one may not be able to control the content or the trend of discussions on the social network, the marketer can definitely influence and guide the discussions. Building a brand image and reputation does take a long time and the Organization needs to have sustained interest and involvement with the blogging community.

Understanding the Power of Feedback and Content on Social Network

Social Web is of the people, by the people and for the people. It is the freedom of expression and freedom of publishing, creating and sharing content using text, audio and visual media that powers the Social Media Networks. There are millions of social networks and the numbers are only growing. For the first time, the marketers and advertising agencies as well as PR agencies have had to admit that they do not control the content that is created on the Social Web. Can any Marketing Organization that is creating and promoting a brand or service afford to ignore and keep away from Social Networks?. It is not possible. Marketers will realize that their competition is present and is participating in the community discussions and therefore you have to be there too. Not only the competition, it is more important for the Organization to realize that the social media network community consists of Satisfied as well as unsatisfied customers and the prospective customers as well. It is important at this stage to remember that the **feedback generated and given by the existing customers and their opinions are likely to influence the 'To be' or 'Would be' customers**.

If you thought that the management slogan of 'Customer is the King' need not be taken seriously, it is time to sit up and take note of the slogan and believe in it seriously. **Social Networks are the most effective and powerful platforms that provide the real feedback from the Customers and this feedback is of immense value to the Companies**. Tech Savvy individuals who are participating in the community discussions regarding your product or service are likely to evaluate your product as soon as it is introduced in the market and give their feedback using visual media in the form of photos or video clippings which can be uploaded into the web in an instant and is made available to all viewers across the globe.

At this point, it is important for the Organizations to realize the potential that such Social Networks hold to make or break their reputation. Any blogger who happens to check into a hotel in any city can immediately post a review of the hotel and his experience adding photographs to prove his statements within a few minutes. Be it favorable or unfavorable, his comments and posts are likely to be viewed and discussed by thousands of viewers who are likely to form their opinions either for or against the hotel. If the experience has not been favorable, the potential of damage can be huge as all the viewers and participants are likely to make a note and avoid the hotel in the future. Even those who are looking for information and reviews about the hotel in particular are likely to get influenced by the unfavorable post causing immense damage to the hotel's business prospects.

The Organizations would do well to understand the power of the Social web and understand that the Social Networks expose the gap between the promise made and the actual delivery against expectation if any. Similarly a satisfied customer's report can also impact the Organization in a huge way. Whether the Customer experience has been positive or negative, the posts are likely to be viewed by thousands in a few minutes and make up their mind regarding future purchase or consumption of your product or service.

Before embarking on branding or marketing exercise on the Social networks, it is important for Organizations to get their act together and ensure that whatever the marketing promises, the operations is geared up and ready to deliver the same. Any shortfall or gap is likely to get highlighted with magnifying effect and influence the potential customers. To undo such damage is likely to take a very long time and a lot of effort.

Social Network Feedback Analysis

As a marketer, it doesn't take one long to understand the high impact and the potential of the Social Media Networks on your business. You will also recognize the fact that the content on the Social Networks is not under your control and it is essentially this freedom of expression and uploading of content that gives the Social Network its huge popularity and growth. Companies engage professional consultants to create and sustain online communities and thus develop a buzz around their new product launches or promotional campaigns. But building reputation for the product as well as for your company calls for sustained involvement and participation in the Social Networks where your existing as well as prospective customers are available.

Discussions and posts on the Social Networks hold a mirror to the promises that the Organization has made and the actual delivery that it has affected. In other words, the platform highlights the difference between the customer expectation built and the actual experience delivered to them. Companies would do well to listen, see and understand such feedbacks and act on them to ensure the shortfalls are covered.

The feedback from the Social Networks can provide a lot of information and data to the Marketers and Organizations which can be used in product development, effective customer service and all other areas that concern the customers. To gather the right feedback, one needs to analyze the information gathered from the Network discussions in detail and methodically tabulate the data. You will find the feedback from the customers in several forms including text messages or posts, audio clips, visuals in the form of photos or videos etc. All of these need to be collated, analyzed with reference to the customer feedback.

Before attempting to analyze the customer feedback from the Social Network content, it is important to establish or answer several questions internally. First and foremost one needs to identify and define the basic promise that the Organization stands committed to. Secondly it is important to state the perceived needs and expectations of the customer and explain how the promise is able to address the customer expectations. Based on these two points, the list of objectives can be further developed to include the actual delivery and point of sale experience, communication process with the customer both in terms of during the sale and post sale service. It would be apt to assign a value for each of the promises made with reference to its relevance to the customers and measure the same. Lastly define the various departments that are likely to gain from the feedback analysis and note down their requirements.

Once the feedback analysis scope and method has been defined, the feedback data may be analyzed and trends identified. Such feedback analysis would be of immense value to Marketing, Advertising, Customer Service as well as the R&D and Product development team besides the Operations departments.

Social Media Channel and Tools

Social Media Channels contain thousands of websites, blogs, forums, videos and so on. Individuals have now begun to spend most of their free time online catching up with various conversations and topics of their interest. When one wishes to get the latest update on news, entertainment, movies, music as well as catch up with what is happening in a particular community of interest as well as catching up with friends and forums besides checking out for new product releases etc where will he find the time to browse through all the sites day after day?. Well this is where the RSS Feeds and other services come into picture. Combined with services like Seesmic, FriendFeed, Twitter and Flickr uploads etc, the people get to know the latest post, the latest content as well as the latest updates on the other communities and networks of their interest as well as of their friends, products and so on. Such services are able to filter information and content as the individual wants it and bring the latest update to him on his mobile at all times. Though the individual has subscribed to hundreds of sites, they do not visit each site all the time to check out the information, rather they use the feeds to alert and bring them the latest updates and deliver them in more meaningful and organized manner.

As a marketer, it is not enough for you to be present in social networks and participate in Social interactions through building your own blogs, forums and so on. You will need to use these social content tools to keep your customers and those that are interested in your products and services updated with the latest news and information that you are putting up as content, least they miss out on visiting your site and checking out the news. Similarly using feeds you can also keep a watch on what your competitors are up to and get a feel of the mood of the market too. Imagine your customers having subscribed to over a hundred different forums and platforms. They are unlikely to keep a watch on and check out what is happening on your site and might miss out on a product safety announcement that you might have made recently. By making use of feeds and instant messages, you are able to bring this important information to your customer's attention and thereby enhance his product awareness which is sure to result in increased loyalty to your product as well.

Events and calendars too can be very creatively used by the marketers to provide very useful information to the interested customers about the various events that they have planned. By giving details of date, time, place, event details etc you can cajole the customer to attend the event be it a sale or a promo event. It would be worthwhile spending some time and checking out the various sophisticated tools and services that are available on the social media channels. Check out services like last.fm contains features that enable it to keep a track of the music that you liked or listened to through I tunes etc and accordingly provides you with calendars and events of artists that you are likely to be interested in. Similar such services are available with many others like Yahoo with their Eventful and Upcoming which lets the customers demand a particular event from you and you can in turn confirm their demand. Such options help you get closer to the niche customers who are listening and following you.

Technology has brought about multi-media capabilities and many advanced communication applications and tools that enable you to connect with your customers and send them audio, video, photo as well as text updates instantaneously and make sure that you get their attention.

The more you invest on understanding the capabilities of the social media channels, the better you will be at trying out a mix of channels and tools to build an effective marketing communication strategy.

Using Social Media Channels with Multiple Business Objectives

Social Media Marketing is the latest game in marketing. Whether you have a product or a service to market, you have no option but to be present in various social media channels for this is where your existing and prospective customers are. More importantly your customers are talking and sharing their ideas, experiences and information that includes reference to your products and services too.

Multi Media technology has fuelled the growth of Social Media channels including blogs, micro blogs, audio & video sharing and Podcasts etc. When it comes to advertising on the Social Media Channels, you will find the pop ups and banners etc to be the same as the traditional media advertising which is interruptive. However from a marketing angle you need not look at Social Media channels only for advertising. There is a lot more that you can do on a larger scale by connecting with your customers, building your image, online reputation as well as benefitting from the interactions that you elicit from the audience regarding your product and services.

Leveraging on Collective Intelligence of the Community

In fact most of the technology businesses have found it extremely useful to blog and connect with the audience, wherein they are able to talk about their product innovations, technology platforms and gain useful insights and assistance from the community in developing as well as getting directions for building the products for the future. Technology is changing very fast and lifecycle of products too is very short. In such situation, being able to feel the pulse of the actual users, interacting with and giving the audience a feel of the product, banking on collective intelligence of the community in solving product or technology related problems can prove highly beneficial for business. No technocrat can ignore the fact that you are able to bank on not just limited brains of your team but of the best talent available in the community. Many times online discussions have paved way to solving major problems faced during product development.

It helps then, to recognize the fact that the concept of marketing and advertising using social media channels is different. You can have several goals while drawing up your strategy for using Social Media channels. Advertising and connecting with your prospective customers is definitely one of the primary motives behind the entire exercise. In addition to doing so, you can also use the channels for very many other goals which may include qualitative as well as quantitative goals too. From using the channels for internal purpose to connect with employees and support vendors, to informing the interested community regarding proposed product development as well as talking about the future course of growth for the Company and eliciting responses from the community on what they think, the Social Media channel can be used as a mirror that reflects your business, your reputation and your customer's behavior, understanding, needs, opinions and feedback etc.

Use Multiple Channels with different Marketing Objectives

Depending upon your strategy and focus, you would need to choose appropriate channel that suits the purpose. **Understanding the different platforms is essential to**

be able to decide on the mix and match of channels that you choose to be present in and participate. Apart from Social Networks including Business and professional Networks and White Label communities, you will find it necessary to be present in the sphere of blogs and other multi-media channels including video sharing and podcasts too. Each of the channels suite a different purpose and give you a chance to connect with the customers on an interactive mode.

Realizing the fact that you are tapping into and interacting with your customers who are the audience on these channels makes you realize the vast amount of opportunities that open up to you to further your business interest. Compare this to just buying advertisement space on the channels where the audience has a choice to bypass and ignore your advertisement, you will realize that the Social Media channels are a gold mine and you couldn't have asked for a better opportunity to be able to reach out and interact with your customers.

Understanding Social Media Holds Key to Building Online Reputation

Difference between Traditional Advertising and Online Advertising on Social Media

When it comes to Advertising in traditional media, the advertisers tend to focus on how to reach the masses at large. However when one looks at the Social Media and plans to design advertising, it becomes important to understand some of the basic differences that make Social Media different from the traditional media. In the traditional media, the advertisements are largely interruptive. People are used to the commercial breaks and the interruptive advertisements amidst the shows. However when it concerns the social media, the major difference to be noted is that the audience does not appreciate interruptive advertising. In fact **the audiences on the internet have several options of being able to install filters, block senders, use pop up blockers and soft wares that block the advertisements on the browser**. What does this mean to the advertisers and marketers. This means that the way to reach out and connect with the internet community has got to be different.

Secondly it also means that the audience does not appreciate being spoken to without permission. There is also the real possibility that in near future one would need to seek similar permission from the prospective customers even to contact them on telephone or through other means of communication.

Therefore it is time for the marketers to sense the changes and anticipate the changing trends that are to come in the near future. As the controls lie with the participants in the social media web, the advertisers and marketers would need to ask for permission to communicate with each prospective audience. More importantly to be able to participate in the social networks and discussions, one would need to be invited. The marketer or the advertiser does not control the participation or the discussion on the social media. Participating or absenting from the Social media and networks is not something that can be easily decided by the Marketer. If the audience is talking about the products or services that the marketer is interested in providing, he has not option but to be present and participate in the online discussions. On the other hand, ignoring and absenting from the online communities can send wrong signals and promote negative sentiments amongst the community.

Building Online Reputation

Understanding the above would help the markers redraw their strategies of using social media for their marketing efforts and build their online reputation. The fact that the audience or the participants control the conversation on the social web also means that the way they perceive your advertising effort would in turn make or break your online reputation. It does not matter how long you have been in business or your position in the market, in the online world, it is your interactions with the community and their perception that determines your reputation.

Building your online reputation is not simple and cannot be done overnight. It has got to be built with sustained and planned online activity and participation as well as with the clear understanding of the participant communities' characteristics as well as the trends. Measuring and studying the social media and the communities that are your captive audience helps design an effective strategy for building online reputation. Social Media marketing agencies offer tailor made as well as custom designed metrics that provide the markets with detailed feedback on the traffic, page views, the dwell in times etc. Several qualitative measures are also able to provide valuable clue on the content, the reviews, the moods and sentiments of the participants. All these feedbacks enable the advertisers to come up with accurate plan to build sustainable online reputation. The feedbacks are critical to manage, grow as well as change or tweak the online reputation and manage the trends over a period of time.

Blogging as Marketing Communication Channel

There is so much happening on the Social Network Marketing scene that Companies now have no option or choice but to be present in these channels. If you are planning to introduce a new product in the market or to build your brand image or reputation, the most preferred option available today happens to be the Social Media Channels.

It is true that you do not have an option but to take part and interact with your customers through those Social Media Channels where they are present. However the medium consists of a whole lot of platforms and channels that can be classified under Social Networks, Social Content and Social Interaction channels. To build an effective marketing communication strategy you would need to be present not in any one but in multiple channels depending upon the presence of your customers.

Blogging happens to be one of the easiest and simplest methods of establishing rapport with your prospective and existing customer base. Blogging includes several categories including personal blogs, Company Blogs, Micro blogging, Photo/Video Sharing and Podcasts.

Blogging - Two Way Communication

Blogging provides one of the easiest, fastest and direct ways of interacting with your audience. By creating and writing your blog, you are able to tell your customers and audience the things that you wish to tell about yourself, your product or service and your company and invite them to share their opinions and feedback etc. Blogging is an initiative from your end and you can choose the amount of time and attention you wish to pay to your blog and build social interactions. Blogging gives you a chance to elicit fair and frank discussion and opinions from the audience and community that is definitely interested in you and your product.

Blogging is not only about you talking about yourself and your product. You will get to listen and understand all about your customers too. Blogging also provides you with the opportunity to listen to your customers, to understand their expectations, their experiences as well as their feelings etc which can give you substantial insight into your own business or product and the way forward in your business. You can manage to cultivate a very close relationship with those who are able to provide you with honest feedback and build a loyal base too.

Blogging is not Advertising

The concept of blogging works different when compared to the other mediums that you use for advertising. In blogging, you are marketing to the customers but not through direct advertisements and one sided messages, but more importantly by listening to your audience, building a relationship with them, taking their feedback and trying to improve your product offering and services. You can use this medium to enhance the value that you provide to your customers. Using this medium involves listening and engaging customers in conversation as against direct advertising. Needless to say that you would need to match up with product performance and service delivery to match with the customer expectation and keep up your promised delivery too.

One of the rules that you have got to remember and follow at all times while blogging is to be transparent and open with information. If you are seriously interested in building a long term profile and reputation, it is best to avoid 'paid blogging' as many of the Companies do. It is better to remember that the blogger community is smart enough to be able to distinguish actual blogging from paid blogging. Any such issue can result in negative publicity which is to be avoided at any cost. Remember at all times that it is best to be open and transparent about facts regarding yourself and your business at all times. It helps to give your profile details and get your audience to know you as a person. Such transparency helps build your image and reputation online.

Different Types of Blogs

Blogging is one of the easiest and simplest ways of reaching out to your audience using the Social Media. Blogging happens to be a very effective medium for building your reputation, for interacting with your customers, for building relationships as well as for business purposes. Blogging entails not only talking about yourself, your ideas, views and opinions, but more importantly to listening to the community of customers who are interested in your and your product. By listening, you get to learn and receive more information and feedback that is likely to help you with your business and product development as well.

In this section, we shall briefly review different types of blogs that are available in Social Media Channels today. Popular types of blogs include Personal blogs, Corporate Blogs, Micro Blogging as well as Blogs by Genre, by Media Type or Device type etc.

Personal Blogs

Check out some of the famous personal blogs of Techies, Investment Bankers, Celebrities or Political Leaders etc and you will get to see the way they have built an online reputation by communicating with audience through their personal blogs. By establishing their persona blogs, they are able to talk and convey their ideas, their opinions and plans to the audience easily. They are also able to elicit response and opinions from the expert community which is equally talented and is able to provide valuable feedback. Such response and being able to read the pulse of the audience, would be of immense value to a political leader or a business entrepreneur.

Personal bloggers make it a point to share some information about themselves, their families, their attitude, lifestyle, likes and dislikes as well as the causes that are close to one's heart etc. Such disclosure helps connect with the audience and gives a picture of the blogger as an individual. This helps connect with likeminded people and sends out a message of transparency as well as honesty, thus contributing to building a public reputation in the long run.

Corporate Blogs

All of the Corporate Companies in the world today have engaged themselves in building and interacting with customers across the globe through their Corporate Blogs. Each of the blogs are created and revolve around the vision and goal that the program is built to support. The goals and vision is again centered on the type of business and the corporate goals too.

In the technology field, you can find the best blog sites maintained by Corporates like IBM, Dell, SAP, Oracle etc. The subjects that are discussed vary from discussions on product, installations, service, applications, problem solving to new developments and several technology related issues, besides customer service etc.

In the service sector, one of the best known blogs belong to South West airlines which is used by the airlines to listen and learn from the actual experiences of the travelers, to communicate, clarify and to announce new service features, promotions, additions and customer care programs as well as to connect with its employees and more importantly to build loyalty amongst the customers. Starbucks is another favorite site of bloggers who not only love the Coffee Experience but find it engaging to contribute to 'My Starbuck Idea'. Starbuck has successfully engaged the customer community across the globe to have a say in the way it spearheads its business in the future. This is one way of building successful and sure shot future.

Other Types of Blogs

Besides the Personal and Corporate Blogs, one other types of blogs that you would want to check out would be the blogs that are built around a particular topic or genre which attracts contributions from the best amongst the community. Political blogs, travel blogs, blogs floated by Scientist community, Educationists and other such specialist blogs. TED Blog is an ideal example of a blog of think tank community where in the best of thinkers put forward their thoughts and the discussions build around the progressive ideas.

What are Micro Blogs ? - All about Micro Blogs

You must have heard it from one and all that no Company has a choice when it comes to being present and marketing through Social Media Channels. Understanding of the various media channels, their capabilities, the kind of audience and community that participates in a particular platform helps in designing or choosing the right mix of media platforms and channels for one's marketing strategy using Social Media Channels.

Social Networks, Social Interaction and Social Content are some of the broad categories of Social Media Channels. In the Social Content category are covered the various types of blogs, audio and video sharing, micro blogs as well as podcasts etc.

Blogs are an effective medium for marketers to use as a platform or a sounding board to talk about themselves, their Company, their philosophy and values in addition to their ideas, their product and services etc. By listening to and sharing interaction with the audience, they can gather informative ideas and suggestions that help future product development as well as build an online reputation and brand loyalty.

What Are Micro Blogs

Micro blogging refers to a type of blogging that uses very quick, small and short messages either in audio, text or video forms. As the name implies, the messages are very short and crisp and usually refer to an present event, a comment about an event and broadcasting of a news clip etc. Though instant text messaging is the most popular form of micro blogging, video clips are also fast becoming popular too.

Micro Blogs - Powerful Medium

Micro blogging has tremendous capacity and capability to relay news instantaneously. Unleashing this power can be of great value to marketers. The power of micro blogging is evident in the cases where news of any international political event or a catastrophe is relayed to the entire world in an instant, even before the same is picked up by the news or TV media or is officially announced.

Twitter, is perhaps the most famous micro blogging medium that has caught the fancy of people all across the world. Besides this there are several services such as

Jaiku, Seesmic as well as Status updates in Facebook, My Space, Google+, Google Buzz etc. are the best examples of Micro blogging services.

Subscribing to micro blogging is very fast and easy. All you need to do is to register with a site like Twitter which shouldn't take you more than a few minutes. Then it takes a few minutes for you to search for your favorite micro blog sites and click follow. Check out your contact list and navigate through to build your contacts through sending invites to friends and interested audience. By posting your own tweets on any interesting topic, event, thought or information that is likely to be of interest to your audience, you can post tweets and those interested will begin to follow you and the link keeps building.

Audio & Video Podcasting

As the technology is evolving, the social media channels to have adapted to multi-media technology. The latest in the Micro blogging platform are the pod casts and video messages. It is no doubt that audio and video contents especially a video can deliver a message more effectively than a simple text message.

Podcasts are nothing but the channel of delivering audio message to the interested community/audience.

What makes podcasts different is that the delivery mode of the podcasts. Podcasts consist of recorded audio files that are delivered to the subscribers device. The subscriber then has the freedom to choose the time and place when he would wish to listen to the broadcast. The point to be noted here is that the choice of engagement lies with the audience and not the originator of the message or the marketer.

Providing information to the audience, customers or subscribers using a video clipping or short film is also possible through micro blogging. A picture can say a thousand things more effectively than a text message and it is able to capture the attention of the audience instantly. This medium when used effectively can be most powerful in spreading awareness, brand building and building loyalty of the customers as well as in helping the prospective customers make up their mind to go for your product. The power of the visual medium can be seen when instant videos of customers talking about their live experiences about an airline, hotel or any product is circulated amongst the members of the community. Such video clips show the actual reality and are effect the community a lot more than text messages and thus engage them instantly.

Going through YouTube as well as other videos of commercial business organizations like Home Depot or Charity etc provide valuable clue and understanding of how to use micro blogs effectively. Micro blogs, especially the podcasts and videos are being used by Social sector, NGOs as well as health and education sector etc very effectively for, the medium lends itself to a global delivery at negligible costs.

At the end, it is helpful for the marketers to remember that these Social Media channels hold great influencing power as well as contributory power of millions, not to forget their global impact and reach.

Social Media and Quantitative Tools

Social Media Marketing has rewritten the marketing methods and theories like never before. Technology has enabled online marketing. When we refer to selling online we mean E-Commerce but when we refer to using Social Media Channels for marketing purposes we are essentially referring to advertising and marketing to customers through the different platforms.

Availability of multiple platforms, multi media options as well as various marketing tools makes Social Media Channels highly interactive with the customers.

Use of quantitative tools like Ratings, Reviews and Recommendations as well as other scoring methods like voting etc are highly beneficial in engaging the customers as well as getting to know what they think about you and your products and such feedback can be highly valuable to any marketer.

Recommendations

If you look at the way that we all behave while deciding to buy any product, you will see that invariably we wish to check with friends and family, especially with someone who has the knowledge of the product or has used the product to see what he or she thinks. In marketing language we call them the influencers. If someone you trust or someone who is an authority on the subject happens to recommend you a particular product, you are likely to go ahead and make that choice in favor of the recommended product.

In the case of Social Media Channels too, innovative options of Rating, Voting, writing Reviews and Recommendations are in vogue. Check out the various websites and channels and see the various kinds of options that are available for recommending a product. Popular methods used are very simple systems like clicking on Thumbs Up or Thumbs Down or using options like 'Digg' etc. Then there are the Net Promoter Scores too that are employed to show the degree of recommendation.

Recommendations from an already customer or an authority carries a lot of weight. From another view point, the number of recommendations can mean a higher rating too. When people start recommending your product and are ready to make their opinion known, you are building a community of people who are willing to pledge their loyalty to you.

Offering Recommendation option can send out the right message to the customers and those who are watching you online. Allowing the community to speak about you shows well on your part and adds weight age to your online presence as well as reputation. Just like how the referral system works in case of pharmaceuticals and other products, recommendations too add weight age to your product in the particular category.

Now days all product catalogues and online selling sites provide recommendation options as a standard tool while many other sites offer voting options. Voting can be used in lieu of rating or recommending a particular product and one can also use description based voting too. Recommendations can also be qualifying in the form of - Recommend, Highly Recommend and so on.

Those who are learning about Social Media Channels and marketing will also do well to know that there are several agencies and professional content providers who are available for writing reviews and recommendations etc on commercial basis. Using such methods to augment the ratings and reviews will not pay in the long run for the user community is smart enough to realize the same in no time. The paid for content can easily be detected by an experienced blogger or surfer. Such gimmicks will bring down the online reputation of the product and the promoter over a period of time. Social Media Channels are very conscious of the social mannerisms, online behavior as well as ethical and moral standards that are upheld on the various platforms.

Use of Quantitative Tools in Social Media Channels

E Commerce, online brand building and marketing using Social Media Channels is one of the most modern developments in Sales and Marketing fields. In fact no business can afford to ignore or be absent from this medium. As long as your audience and customers are present and discussing about their experiences about your product or your competitor's products and services, you will need to be present there.

Social Media consists of various platforms that are grouped loosely under Social Networks, Social Content and Social Interactions. In this section, we will be exploring the employability of some of the quantitative tools such as Ratings, Reviews and Recommendations in Social Media Marketing, with an aim to understand the utility of these tools from a marketing perspective.

Quantitative Tools are Helpful to Marketers

A look at Social Media channels gives us a feeling that the same applies to and consists of individuals who contribute their experiences, opinions and such contributions leads to building a content that is based on consensus. While this is largely true, the same can also be viewed from a entirely different perspective of that of a marketer and to use the same channels and discussions to build a relationship with the customers, to build brand awareness and loyalty and finally to influence the prospective customer to buy your product or service.

If you think that the Social Networks and other media are all related to personal discussions and subjects, you may be right. But go through all of the content that is generated in the various channels. You will see a lot of discussions taking place about politics, news, economy as well as about health, travel and more importantly about the personal and recent experiences of the people. Such discussions about one's experience and the other's discussions, comments etc will always include their experience of a product or a service that they recently engaged with. Chances are that the products could be yours or your competitors. Alternatively you might want to explore the platforms to see where the community is talking about the products that you are interested in and dealing with and target that particular community to build your program further.

Application of Quantitative tools such as Ratings, Recommendations and other such tools as a part of your online marketing efforts are useful to you as the

marketer as well as to the audience. As a marketer you get a chance to listen to what your customers are saying about your product and your competitor's products as well. You can use the insight gained to improve your product further and also enhance the experience for the customers. Precise information gathered from the qualitative tools can tell you a lot about what your customer likes, what he doesn't like and what he finds useful etc. Imagine what this feedback can do to improve your product and your business.

Customers Benefit from Online Quantitative Tools

The online ratings tools help advertise your product effortlessly to the new audience and prospective customers as well. When a customer is in the process of building awareness and gathering information to make a decision to purchase, he is likely to bank heavily upon the ratings and recommendations of other users. Traditionally word of mouth publicity has always been an effective medium. So also in case of Social Media, the recommendations and ratings are effective in helping the prospective customer sway his decision to buy your product.

Though the quantitative tools appear very effective and useful, caution has to be exercised in managing and controlling the same, for without effective controls in place you might end up inviting unwarranted feedback/advice that might be harmful for your reputation.

To understand the effectiveness and modalities of the application of quantitative tools, take some time to study various sites that offer ratings, reviews and recommendations and make a list of your observations as to how they are useful to the audience, to you as the marketer as well as how to introduce, monitor and control the entire online process.

Usage of Quantitative Tools in Social Content

Social Media as a platform for marketing provides for continuous innovation, thanks to the evolving technology. No other medium gives you the kind of direct and interactive opportunity as do the Social Media Channels. Though the medium is seen to be belonging largely to the audience who discuss, participate and contribute to creating content, online marketing using the same platform has gone places. Today no brand worth its name can afford to ignore or absent itself from the platform where its customers are present and are discussing about their preferences, likes, dislikes and experiences etc.

As in the case of traditional media, Social Media too developed the concepts of online advertisements which continues to exist and grow in the form of pop ups, banners and other multi-media clippings. Online advertising works out to be very cheap and at the same time has the capability to reach out to larger audience. In the second phase developers introduced embedded marketing applications that engage the customer directly and let him tell what he thinks of your product. Use of quantitative tools such as Ratings, Recommendations and Reviews have become highly effective means of giving the voice to customer's opinions, preferences and feedbacks.

It helps to understand briefly how these Quantitative tools work in the context of both the customers as well as the marketers.

Ratings

Check out any information about any product or service on the Social Networks and you will see the ratings that appear below the same. Books, photos, Hotels and movies etc are some of the most popular categories which are rated by the audience.

Providing a mechanism and asking the audience to rate the particular offer, product or service is one of the most popular ways of measuring what the customers think of the same. It reflects the overall opinion of the audience with respect of their expectation of the product or service and with respect to what or how the product/service is expected to perform.

A highly rated movie tends to build into a buzz and the publicity around the same tends to spread faster and wider within a short period of time. Many people who wish to watch a movie over the weekend are likely to look for the ratings and choose the movie accordingly. If you check out the movie ratings system, you will normally see five stars being used for rating the movie from excellent to good, three stars for an average move, and so on. It is quite likely that you will not bother to check out the movies that have below two star ranking.

Ratings can be a good barometer of how well the product is accepted and liked by your customers and it also measures the fulfillment of Customer Expectations. On the marketing front, the ratings speak for your product and it is there for all others to see. Just like word of mouth publicity, the ratings too help in bringing you publicity which is good or bad depending upon your product performance. This is not all, rankings help you to gauge the customer's moods and expectations better. You get to listen and watch your customers talking about your product as well as your competitor's product as well and such information about your competition can give you very many insights into your business.

It is quite likely that many marketers would shy away from getting anywhere near using such ratings and other tools. This can only mean that they are missing out on opportunities of getting valuable feedback as well as publicity. As long as the aim is to receive and act on the feedback and to work on making your product offering better, there is no need for any hesitation in using such feedback mechanisms.

Social Media Channels - Categorization

When one looks at the various social media channels and the traffic that flows through the various networks, you will be surprised at the amount of conversation and exchange of information that is taking place. As an individual it is but natural that every one of us would be logging in to several networks almost on daily basis and pursuing our interests. When you wish to study Social Media from the perspective of a marketer interested in reaching out to the larger audience which happens to be your prospective customers, you will find that your approach to understanding of the Social Media needs to change. Essentially you have got to change your perception from that of a Social Network user or participant to that of a Marketer which calls for looking at the Social Media from a different angle altogether.

Social Media channels can be grouped together under broad functional categories such as Platforms, Content and Networks promoting interaction. By listing all of the platforms under the said categories help the marketer to choose his channel mix appropriately.

It helps one to understand and identify the prospective customers and obtain clarity on how to engage with the customer positively. By identifying the particular medium that is likely to be effective in reaching out to the prospective customer and prompting him to make that decision to buy you are able to build and apply specific customer centric approach and successfully reach the target audience.

Social Platforms category includes so called White Label Social Networks, Personal Social Networks as well as Wikis etc. Under Social Content, the various blogs, micro blogs, video sharing, photos as well as audio and podcast etc are covered. Social interaction platforms include the SMS, Emails, RSS as well as the various events etc.

Marketing programs at a macro level deal with the overall strategy. The media plan too contains a larger frame work of approach to using various media including print, visual and traditional media. Social Media cannot be used in isolation and it forms a subset or a part of the overall media mix that the advertiser uses to approach the consumers.

From amongst the various social media channels, it is important to identify that particular segment of target audience, map their presence in the particular platform and then choose the appropriate method of participation. Mapping the social feedback cycle, understanding how the prospective customer makes his decision with the help of the others participating in the social media is necessary to be able to build a specific social media strategy. Social interaction forms the basis of advertising and marketing.

Word of mouth publicity tends to play a significant role in the traditional marketing and sales channels. When it comes to Social Media, the Word of Mouth assumes gigantic proportion especially in case of micro blogging, SMS and other channels. Understanding how this can aid or harm the marketer's reputation on the Social Media helps one design an effective marketing strategy that is tailor made for this segment.

Identifying Marketing Opportunity through Social Networks

When you are interested in building a Social Media Plan as a part of your larger marketing program, you will need to understand all about the various Social Media channels and only then will you be able to arrive at a mix of channels and mediums that are provide the right opportunity for you to build your online reputation.

Internet Usage - Then and Now

Ever since internet brought the world closer, a new culture or lifestyle has evolved around the net. In the early stages, with limited bandwidth, connectivity and slower speeds, individuals logged on to the net from time to time to check emails, to check out different information that they found useful. With availability of higher speed and bandwidth people began to log in to play games, watch news, study and invest into the stock market etc. This meant that the time they spent using the internet increased significantly. Now if you review the scene, you will find that most homes and offices have their internet connections 'On' all through the day and people are beginning to depend upon the internet for a lot more things including shopping, entertainment and majorly into interacting and socializing with friends. Thus Social Networks have become a part and parcel of daily living. Every individual tends to be a part of one or several social networks and online communities which he keeps getting into and checking out from time to time.

TV & Print Media Advertisements

What does the above development mean to an advertiser or a marketing professional?. At this juncture it helps to understand a bit of the psyche of individuals and their online behavior. It is a well known common fact that advertisements on the TV and Print media are ignored largely by the audience. It is at the time of a commercial break that people choose to move away from the TV to attend to their personal needs and come back to watching TV when the actual program begins again. Everyone considers TV advertisements to be an unwelcome interruption over which they have no control.

Advertising & Building Brand through Social Networks

In the social networks, there are several opportunities for placing advertisement banners and pop ups. It is possible to build a media rich and interactive advertisement banner and exhibit it prominently on Google, My Space and other important sites. Besides you can also use the embedded marketing applications that are available on various sites to build your brand image.

As compared to TV and other mediums, online advertisements have a better chance of being viewed by the audience as they are placed on the websites which one is visiting. However the fact that individuals do get to see the ad banners a little longer than their viewing of TV and other advertisements need not contribute to building a significant brand image. At the most, it might help build a awareness or brand recall.

The real game changer for the advertiser would be the social network communities and their discussions that are taking place all the time. A smart social media expert understands the context of the online community and be able to feel the pulse of the audience. When he understands that the participants are taking part in social interaction and that everyone is interested in contributing to the discussion as well as listening to others, finding facts, sharing opinions etc, he sees the opportunity to be able to match the needs of the online community with the content that he is able to provide. When you are able to provide transparent and useful facts or content, you will find the community engaging in continuous conversations and discussions with you. When they find that your contributions are of use to them and help them, they are likely to become your customers and can become evangelists as well. Therefore participating in the discussions, influencing the discussions and opinions while continuing to respect the values and beliefs that the community holds together would become your game plan. This then is the most important and direct opportunity that you as a marketing professional would get to connect with your target audience, to cultivate relationship, to help convert opportunities into sales and more importantly build a reputation for your brand as well as your Company.

Apart from the direct online participation, you can also use some of the marketing applications that come with the Social Networks. From the entertainment based applications including Sneding Karma, Vampire Bites to Social Vibe, Graffiti Wall and Product Pulse can be effective in helping you build your online reputation consistently.

Using Business and Social Networks for Marketing & Organizational Purposes

As a part of advertising campaign or marketing program, every business will need to use Social Media channels to connect with the market, the prospective Customer as well as the 'Already' Customer. If you are interested in building a brand and an image for your product as well as for your Organization or business, you have no option but to be present on the Social Media. Social Media consists of various channels and platforms grouped under Social Networks, Social Content and Social Interactions.

In this section, we are focusing on Social Networks including the Personal Social Networks as well as Professional/Business Networks and White Label Networks. Social Networks provide a huge opportunity for an Organization to connect with a community that is interested in the line of business or the product that the Organization is talking about build an online reputation in the long run.

Building Internal Social Networks Within the Organization

Organizations have found it very profitable to participate and build Social Networks not only with the outside community but within the organization including all the employees. By encouraging, listening and participating in discussions with the employee community, the Organization is able to promote a non formal platform that encourages the employees to speak up about their views, problems. Important feedback on what the employees think of a particular product, policy or the Company can be gathered easily on such social networks. These networks help the Organizations to search for and recruit good talent as well as nurture smart talent too. Internal Social Networks help the Organization feel the pulse of the employees, build and promote an open culture and enhance the feeling of togetherness too. On the marketing front, it helps the Organization announce its future plans for product development, invite productive and creative feedback and assessment as well as build internal loyalty too.

How to Benefit from Participating in Professional & Business Social Networks

Apart from using Personal Social Networks as well as the Internal Social Networks, one can benefit largely from using professional Social Networks too. **Sites like LinkedIn, Face Book and Jigsaw etc, prove to be a huge mine of data and information on various contacts, specific interest groups, communities of experts etc**. Marketers have realized the potential that exists in these business social networks and the community of professionals and have developed successful strategy to engage them for productive purposes. Most of the leading brands and companies have developed strategies of introducing discussions around a new product that they are planning to develop and release and thus build a community of people interested in the said product. By cultivating a online community, they are able to create a buzz around the product and such publicity helps in its actual product launch. In many cases, the Organizations are able to engage with the community of experts on productive discussions regarding the product and thus obtain useful feedback, suggestions and solutions that help with product development. Market research and market feedback can be generated with the help of online communities.

Social Networks, both individual networks as well as professional networks provide the best opportunities for the Organizations to be in continuous touch with its audience and more importantly engage with them on an interactive basis. How far and how much you can get out of these platforms depends upon the how much you can engage consistently and persistently as well as invest time and effort in engaging your customers.

www.ingramcontent.com/pod-product-compliance
Lightning Source LLC
Chambersburg PA
CBHW080814180526
45168CB00006B/2452